Only

Only

POEMS

REBECCA FOUST

FOUR WAY BOOKS
TRIBECA

Library of Congress Cataloging-in-Publication Data

Names: Foust, Rebecca, 1957– author.
Title: Only / Rebecca Foust.
Description: [New York] : [Four Way Books], [2022]
Identifiers: LCCN 2022003883 | ISBN 9781954245297 (paperback) | ISBN 9781954245365 (epub)
Subjects: LCGFT: Poetry.
Classification: LCC PS3606.O846 O55 2022 | DDC 811/.6--dc23/eng/20220209
LC record available at https://lccn.loc.gov/2022003883

This book is manufactured in the United States of America and printed on acid-free paper.

Four Way Books is a not-for-profit literary press. We are grateful for the assistance we receive from individual donors, public arts agencies, and private foundations including the NEA, NEA Cares, Literary Arts Emergency Fund, and the New York State Council on the Arts, a state agency.

We are a proud member of the Community of Literary Magazines and Presses.

CONTENTS

WATERSHED

Notes

Only

Prompt

Write only what you absolutely do not know, not what you're merely not sure of.
STEPHEN DUNN

Null. All. What's after death or before.

Where my old dog is now, my mother,

my father—not the ashes clumped

in a box, but the mad licking

and tail-beating and the gaze,

dense with devotion, of iris-less eyes.

My father's delight in anything

wingless or red, why my mother left

that night, barefoot and worried

she'd miss it, the first landfall migration

of geese in raft after dark raft aloft

in a gray sky, an acre of feather and beak

that boiled and blotted the dark lake,

and no sound but the high cry.

Remember

Dream of the Rood

I wanted to be the girl with the small sharp shears who could balance
a child with a stone, who knelt in a glade

and laid sticks at right angles to build her own house where the violets,
her friends, had tender faces and leaves.

The mines were abandoned, silk mills closed, the railroad reduced
to one line, one long low wail at 2 am.

The town's reason, gone. Stripper pit/strawberries/stripper pit/corn.
Coke-caked smokestacks, brick pink

in morning sun. Hollow train barns, canals silted in. Stores boarded up,
fan windows above still parsing light,

the dance pavilion's million small panes chalked white. Sick rivers
and orchards, stick thickets in ground

gummed with tar. Each corner's bar facing a church, the horizon's broad
band of blue mountains gashed by gravel

where the power went in. Or where, the tale tells, a giant was crushed
by the burst sack of his own greed: each stolen child

replaced by a stone and the sack re-sewn by the last one to leave, a girl
with sharp shears who knew when not to knot the thread.

Woodland paths ferned and footed with teaberry and mayapple, supplicant
moss raising small ochre cups to catch rain,

and always the rain, or clouds sodden with the idea of it, pressing down.
Home was where I went to be alone,

fourteen elbows at table, seven faces in one mirror, a babble and blur
in which each tended his or her own

bright bubble of silence. My mother deep in her book, my father in his bottle
—visions of splintered dry ice, church people

tranced and speaking in tongues—I lived in a world traced by the footprints
of sparrows on snow

but narrated myself an English orphan with imaginary and very small friends.
"Honey, I'm worried for you,"

my mother said. "People like us just get knocked down." My sisters and I ran
in the hot dark to hide, hoping not to be found;

we played Statues; we played games that taught us, when touched, to freeze.
The first poet I recognized had been dead

for twelve centuries when I read what was written in stone, in the language
of tree and pain, and a voice with no name

called out to me, called me alive across time; he or she or they called me,
and I began to remember it all.

Thirteen

I was thirteen, and there was a boy's mouth
where my legs met. My heart beat

like a bird caught in a bag, let's say
for her plumage. I could smell his want,

thirteen and there was a boy, and I became
something salt and sweet

where my legs met. My heart like a bird
swelled and split

the clear air with its song. I was the must,
the first press wine,

thirteen, and only this boy and the needles
under the pines,

that cedar bed, fragrant and ancient as dust
and where my legs met—thirst—

a boy, my heart like a bright, caught bird.

Parts of Speech

We came to a grove and you drew me in;
I wondered about our right to wander
where we would in that wood of old pine,
my hand in yours and yours in mine.
Fair was the raiment of cloud overhead.
Or it was not fair, or it was just
beginning to clear. In truth all I saw
was your face and the white-capped cove,
and the old rowboat we dragged into shore.
In truth, there was no grove, no cove,
no clouds, no scow—the only nouns
being voice, face, and hands—or, the pine
and the wood were just active and aching
verbs. Or, that is all I remember now.

exsultate jubilate

that you were exactly as ardent as I and as novice
that you had to ask only once but did ask
          and did not speak of it after to others

that it was an eclogue and an orchard dialogue
with apples and talking and tears
          and we did not know but learned to know

and learned to know without fear   that you
learned with me   going slow
          and took nothing   but only gave

and received   without shame   in slant light
in the fall   your hands framing my face
          and you kissing me   open-eyed

you laughing into my mouth   our going together
into the great secret exsultate jubilate
          in actual fact then   and now recalled as

Remember

Your eyes speaking your vows, white linen
unwinding ahead of us, shining,
parquet laid on a lawn under old poplars,
fragile white lilies and fat waxen tapers,
a toast from my father furloughed from cancer,
a white-plumed pen and a gilt-edged guest book,
your rented tails, my off-the-rack dress
strewn with seed pearls, the tumult of future
in my morning mirror. Cousins romancing
maiden aunts—dancing, people who *never* danced—
happiness taut in yellow-and-white stripes
against blue sky, and spring still half on the spool.
The runner ahead, unwinding its shining,
and behind us, the shining unwound.

Dawn Piece

after "Night-Piece" by Stanley Kunitz

—and everywhere of a sudden spring, bud-break, birds
purling sixteenth notes,

even the ravens, beach plum in wedding gowns,
and the dune's strict dun

turning chartreuse. Let us return to the rising tide,
you in your endless joyous tattoo,

me in my necklace of blown-glass vowels. Come barefoot
summer: dream late, dream noon

of a red moon swollen by mist and warm rain, dream
of when touch taught

the heart to beat at the throat and under one hipbone,
beat a new meter

of flicker and float, of grace note. Now when I clench
and grind my teeth in my sleep, Love,

believe it is only my mouth seeking the last marrow
memory before night bleeds out

into the neap-tide drawn dawn, and let me sleep on,
Love, let me sleep on.

Cocktail Hour

It's like a nibble
at my line. I do not feel it all the time.

I do not feel it all—
the time just goes more slowly then—

but I do not
feel it all the time. A hair-fine spine

rubbed backward
in my palm—I do not feel it all the time—

& when I do,
it's not so bad, just a nibble at my line,

a swallowed barb, or
like the fish has sunk both its rows

of curving teeth
into my thigh, each gilled breath a tug

as its body lolls & heaves,
a sawtooth edge that frays the line

or cuts the flesh
in scalloped grooves. It sounds so much

worse than it really is,

& I do not feel it all the time—only when

the river moves.

Self-Improvement

Barn's burnt down—now I can see the moon.
MIZUTA MASAHIDE

It's 52 o'clock & the Project of You

has begun anew: quit drinking

again, start jogging. Floss. Get a clue

about what-it-all-means, what you

mean to do. Wake before noon

now & then. Mend the broken yolk

of your mind; bail its sunk boat.

Meditate. And for God's sake, eat

more fruit. See the dentist & proctologist;

have some fun. Commit at least one

unoriginal sin (with a condom, please,

& without a gun). Go to the barn, burn

it down, burn the day. Then you can

see the moon, without yourself in the way.

not the thing but the fossil of the thing

an ammonite's dull weight smells of new snow   a limestone clam
called *brachiopod*   licked   gleams like a dark marble

and tastes of cast-iron bell   its absence of sound & soft parts
perfecting an imperfection of knowledge called faith

bare of the lies told by *the thing itself*   bravado bloom   spilt
perfume   music   bee pollen & blood &

all that hot narcotic blur—these casts and molds resonant as words
& like lunar craters seen best in eclipse

so that when I trace the diamond-on-diamond pattern etched in slate
of the bark that once cloaked a tree   a canopy

spreads overhead   a vine unwinds   buds, blooms & bears fruit
that heaps seeds at my feet   an ancient sea swells

and floods the dry valley below   wet salt to knees   hips
waist   chest   neck   mouth   eyes

&   under my breastbone   a fish leaps

Spring Is

The ideogram for sorrow is called *Autumn Heart*,
but Spring is the season that aches:

green shoots tender as newborns wearing their caps
of dirt crumbs crocheted with snow,

brave crocuses stiff-glistered with frost, and on the cold shore,
oyster spat—each grain a tiny sealed urn

holding a life—left sifted in drifts by the tide. Dante's squalls
of sere, fallen leaves exist only in equipoise

with this surging urge of the dead being born, and here,
the characters agree: The symbol for *Spring* is

layered, the brushstrokes for *wither* and *coffin* still faintly there
beneath those for *horizon, day, sky, leaf,* and *tree.*

Cake

for my mother

You took your long turn to sicken
and thin, honed toward death
and glazed light; bones fine
as Meissen, the merest breath
of teacup barely keeping the shape
of your hot, sweet pour.
But I'm not done, you kept
saying, your tray borne
away, clearing off everything
that gave you pleasure: clotted cream,
buttered crumbs, honey, and ginseng
licked off your thumb,
one last deep drag of dark sweet smoke
—you wanted to have your cake—

Night Skating

after Kafka

I push off and glide
to the center of the dark lake
then head for where
I know the river

feeds in, my blades tracing
moonlit Sanskrit
on the through-the-glass-darkly
daguerreotyped ice.

The way is away
from the voices
and bonfires, the way
is dark and narrow

with trees bending down,
threading bootlaces
with branches to trip me
while I skate to a place

known to only my dead
mother and me. I push
and pump till I find it,
the black ice

doming a deep secret

spring. And now
something is coming apart,
forgetting

how firmly it once was
embodied, a lock
set in concrete
giving way to the moss's

invisible feast. The least
branch succumbs first
to spring, and I glide
through moonlight,

setting my edge, soaring
and swooping
like unchecked error,
the ice a mirror holding me

while it holds my reflection.
I don't want anymore
to hide from myself
where I'm going—

deep into some far and alone
recede where my mother

led me, thirty years gone.
If I keep on,

I know I will get there,
to the dark heart
at the heart of the heart
of this vast, frozen lake.

Lines

Barbara Ann Redline, 1929–1999

Born the last Samuels, Gramma married and went blind.
In her new name, "Redline,"

she bore six daughters and two sons: one drunk without
issue, one gassed in the war.

An engine frozen to two lines of steel, fallow as the field
weeding up all around it. I said *blood*.

I said *yearning*. I spoke of the foundry's dark heart
glowed red, of brick burned

from within and ash spiraled from smokestacks, dark ache
traced on blank blue.

Of grass lifting ties between tracks. Of slow glow of rust.
I said *Redline*. I said *men*

lost in the mine, terminal, end of the line. We are carnage
cleared by the cowcatcher,

we are clay scored by time's plow. You say, *but what*
of the grapevine clotted with fruit,

the fruit pressed into wine, and the bend in the light
where the light bends down? You say

a grandson was born. But I say *the daughters are gone,*
and I say *blood.* I say *my mother.*

I say *yearning furrows my heart in long, straight lines.*

Let Deer

for my uncle

These mountains look like your mountains, bare-tree blurred,
valleys quilted in tussock and shadow

in a world I no longer know. I smell the dark soil and leaf meal
that tomorrow will receive you

three thousand miles to the east, the white clapboard church
with its ceiling of gold stars

picked out against navy blue, and the redbud outside swelled
like an inflamed wound.

Let it be a day like today, sky-rinsed, the mountains sounding
their low, purple chord. Let owls call

after the author of midnight, and trout arc silver over the river.
Let deer come at dusk to the salt block

you set out last fall. Let someone be willing to want your things:
the twenty-three oil pastels of the Shawnee,

the stories and poems never sent off to *Field & Stream*. Let us
remember you as you were before

being swallowed by the bottle, a boy in the woods with a book
and a fly-rod in either hand, and—

Compline

In your dream of what never happened
        a boy turns away from your grief,
and each month's empty womb tolls a compline
        to spring. Once you knew time

as a starving, sumptuous waste
        that felt better than pomegranates
ever could taste. Now, despair
        keen as a blade drawn again and again

in water run over a stone, and so bright
        it might be the fierce start of joy.
You see now what can't be seen by the young
        —the light cast by your own midnight,

mudflats licked to a gleam by the neap tide,
        Gawain hewn but still the tale's hero,
the rood bleeding out into bloom—and you
        learn to love the world as it is: gorgeous
        in its mortal wound.

Only

Only

O Love this happened or it did not.
In a room with green walls

my son was born. The cord was torn
too soon, so they cut off

his head to save his heart. He lived
for a long time.

For a long time there was no breath or cry.
When finally he spoke,

he spoke the wide, whorled leaves of corn.
He spoke the crickets

in clusters beneath the sheaves, he sang
the soil in. He sang the wind

in the dune and hush of ebb tide. Some say
he died. Some say he died.

the unexploded ordnance bin

our son found the hollow shell
snub-nosed & finned
& looking like an Acme cartoon bomb
where we raked for clams
he wanted to keep it
& we wanted to let him

even the old oysterman wanted
to let him   but we'd read about
the shell found & kept
for three weeks by an Oregon boy
before the powder
dried   & it went off

we took a few minutes
to snap photos of our son,
like any ordinary boy then
putting the shell under his sister's pillow
& pretending to launch it
at the foods that made him gag

at the police station
the desk sergeant crooked
a thumb toward the dune
with its big metal bin & warning sign

once a month   he said   we set them off
& it really lights the place up

it's too small to be seen   the gene
that mutates   but I imagine it
anyway with snub nose & fins & powder
waiting to dry   first words
blown off & away like the fingers
of that Oregon boy

whose mom's grief I used to feel safe from
who let her son keep his bomb
in ignorance or faith strong as
my own caution   that led in the end
to the same spectacular
dismemberment of the future

& I wonder   what it would look like
the bin for safe disposal of genes
that some have said & still say
can ruin children   & I think maybe
it's my own body   or rather
the body without children

or rather   the body that's lucky
or belonging to someone still living

in ignorance & improbable faith

or maybe the bin is the world

when it was young   & to be human

was all promise & radiance

unwinding dawn mudflats

into long shining ribbons

pink as a newborn baby's gums

& elsewhere   a family

in a warm illuminated room

is eating steamed clams

or just any ordinary dinner   as if

it weren't going to blow all to hell

any second   all those bright dreams

lit up like tracer fire

over the dark dunes   like the Perseids

only not at all like the Perseids

Collaborator

I could hear something from the kitchen
where I stood paring apples for the pie
planned to mark the moment
of my 10-year-old's playdate, his first
since the move and our first time
with a troop of boys over to trample
the flowerbeds, tear down the old treehouse
and, whooping and laughing,
strip the citrus trees bare. Boys will be boys,
I thought, so so so seduced by the plural—
my son for this day not alone,
but this sound was different.
Not the glorious cacophony
of boys-being-boys, but just one boy—my boy—
lying face down in the dirt
while a hail of green oranges rained down.

I helped him up, wiped his face,
and broke up the circle of boys,
boys with eyes cast down and sometimes
sickled sideways to wink or grin in a way
they thought I couldn't see. I had a choice
then: make a scene and send them home?
Or, somehow allow them to stay?

There was the pie, and the desolate day ahead,

the desolate tomorrow, and the chain

of desolate yesterdays slung slack behind.

There was my son for whom,

it being his first playdate since the move,

this was a normal playdate, and who,

when I asked, said, *You can't*

send them home—they're my friends!

There was the ER Doc who'd told me

to go home where *no one would have to try*

to save him, and his nurse, whose glass voice

asked me twice, *have you ever prayed?*

I needed them on board, and later, the teachers

who wanted to transfer or expel him.

His Sunday-night stomachaches, and the time

I saw him at recess in the bushes, hiding

his eyes so he would not be seen.

So there was all that, and the here-and-now

of a child unable to fathom malice or guile

and able to forgive anyone of anything.

There was also the pie. And, God forgive me,

I let those boys stay.

I practically begged them to stay.

Perseids

When the real star died and fell, I knew the others for tricks,
trompe l'œil on insides of eyelids. But it was no trick
when that star larger than sky fell out of my sky,

shock of arc then black. My son has chest pains again.
When he was young it was easy to hold his hand
all night so he wouldn't die

of trace toxins in cereal or the new mole on his left little toe.
I sang him back to sleep and the next day he was off again,
climbing trees higher than I could reach

or hunching all day over a fixed lens, knotting a fish line
fine as an eyelash. He collected horseshoe crab trash,
knowing and naming each slender spire

I broke one once and hid it, but he missed it later, every piece
consecrated, and constellated among others in precise
patterns in the sky of his bedroom floor.

He's tall now, with a beard. The astral map is in pieces,
just as real stars come unmoored and fall
into flaming swords. Power fails,

EKGs skip and stutter, MRIs hum, then blink off. A boy
he knew in school returns from Iraq without legs.
He trolls the internet for side effects

of medicine taken to decrease the world's discomfort
with him. "Rarely fatal" *doesn't mean never,*
and what logic doesn't whet each day's edge

with fear? *I could die, I might die, we all die. I'll die.*
Maybe tonight, alone in his sleep. *Don't get mad,*
Mom. We've done all the tests twice,

but being alive means proving a negative. So how can
we go on believing each day won't be the one
that flames out? When he walks in his sleep,

his open eyes are dark night-terror pools. Shh, now
he's dropping off, worry lines etching his brow.
Overhead, stars arc across the dark sky
making small curved tears, and the light leaks out.

Everything Golden Is Spilled

You were born and your hour was silver,
new moonlight strewn

on dark ground. Pearls, seeds, wide banks
of clouds, your bright hair,

your damp, sleeping lap-weight, your scalp's
yolky chuff, tug at the nipple,

the universe contracted to suck and glow;
grain, drops of rain,

dreams for a time ripening and bending
like wheat weighted with seed.

When did the season turn? Drained down
now, gone—we are

still in it, but the world has grown old
and I want that bud

of a boy back, packed with what might yet
bloom, each spiraled sepal

still sealed, and nothing, nothing revealed.

Like Birders

Shared obsession and fixed gaze, six of them brood
over three rebuilt monitors.

Taken out to dinner, they speak acronym—RPG, DM,
LCD—the way you might parse

beak sizes and shapes, flight patterns, and the markings
on the breast of a juvenile spotted grouse.

I want to say *read a book, get a job, fall in love, make
anything real happen.* They occupy spots

on a grid penciled on butcher paper. Eyes closed, each boy
plots his plan for survival. Friends drowned

in frozen fens, the enemy everywhere hidden, and burned
is the grail and the ark; but, each hand

is certain, holding the die, knowing by pitch or array of note
which creature roosts, or lurks in the dark.

reflection

afraid   knowing   always
I'll die before you

but in this wild   dark
New Hampshire

meadow   fireflies   glow
like a downed pulsar

throbbing   caught by clouds
& thrown down again

all   incandescence
like your face

&   no trace of errant gene
or what must perish

to breed such rapture light

Saturn-Peach

Yours was an easy birth, daughter,
quick & without forceps or knife
or long savage silence;
you burst the world with a wail,
then sought my breast. Your brain
unbruised, you were intact
& un-anything: -ICU'd, -IV'd,
-EKG'd, -transfused, -gavaged,
or otherwise scanned and perused.
You came home the next day, where
you ate & shat & dreamed
& slept & slept—what they'd always said
babies do—blossom mouth, Saturn-peach
hands, dark hair tufting your ears
& whorled down your doll's spine. I lay
beside you, watching your chest fill & fall,
& measured your breath with my breath,
your foot with my thumb, your thumb
with my eyelash. You smiled on cue,
hitting the benchmarks, & when
I needed help, Dr. Spock (who'd never
been right before) knew just what to do.
You, new, & the world—& everything—
everything new.

Paean

on reading my daughter's soil engineering thesis

A sine wave will go a long way and not fade;
it will be drunk by the roots

of the house, then by the ground: *Surface waves,
Body waves.* And *Love waves*

—*transverse motions perpendicular to the vector
of propagation*—

that is, love is a wave that itself nulls.
It's not the quake that kills,

then, but *subsurface structural failure.* Not the war,
but those who did nothing

to stop it; not the affair, but what the marriage
was not built on.

In *resonance,* soil waves swell when they meet
other waves—a passing train,

crickets that hit the same note at the same time;
then like a great bowl the earth tips,

land masses sliding like pudding to the one side—
and big things fall down and we die.

Big things fall down and we die, and why is always
the question we ask without answer

and still must ask. But you, daughter, with your steel
-toed boots and cans of white spray paint

and little colored flags flying on stakes, you are now
the one holding up the world's buildings

and bridges, and next time I cross one while a train
trundles by, I'll think of Love Waves,

how we thwart what we cherish, how we risk being
too much in tune with the breath

and pulse of the world, and I'll thank physics or God
for the spark that joined spark

to ignite you. And give praise that keeping the world
from flying apart is now less and less my job.

Yes, the tide goes out and waves ebb; in the still hour
the world is withdrawn. But you, Love,

will wave to me from the bridge rampart. You'll be wearing
your hard hat. And you will go on.

Lies I Told My Third Child

The stuffed bear left on the plane did not
really come back home from Curaçao;
the one restored to your frantic hands
was bought at Toys "R" Us and dressed
in sunglasses and tiny Luau shirt by—me.
Polar Bears actually do not, as we told you then,
enjoy tropical weather. And "Baby Billy," who
needed your binkie so much more than you?
He did not exist. I don't know if Christ rose,
but Santa was Dad, and the world is not
your or anyone's oyster to be pried open
and slurped. And it's not true that who you are
—girl or boy—can be usurped by your birth:
people just are. Either. Neither. Sometimes, both.

Abeyance

I made soup tonight, with cabbage, chard
and thyme picked outside our back door.
For this moment the room is warm and light,
and I can presume you safe somewhere.
I know the night lives inside you. I know
we made mistakes, dividing you, and hiding
you from you inside. I know a trans girl
was knifed last week, another set aflame,
and that these things happen all the time.
I know I lack the words, or all the words
I say are wrong. I know I'll call, and you
won't answer, and still I'll call. I want to tell you
you are loved with all I have, recklessly,
and with abandon, loved the way the cabbage
in my garden near-inverts itself, splayed
to catch each last ray of sun. And how
the feeling furling-in only makes the heart
more dense and green. Tonight it seems like
something one could bear.

Guess what, Dad and I finally figured out Pandora,
and after all those years of silence, our old music
fills the air. It fills the air, and somehow, here,

at this instant and for this instant only
—perhaps three bars—what I recall equals all I feel,
and I remember all the words.

Echo

at the gorge in Truchas, NM

The stone fit my hand. Like any promise, it had weight
and a hollow you could drink water from,

or fill with sand. I tucked it inside my vest—baby borne
in a sling, that damp weight on my chest;

the stone was cool and calm, and I felt something flow
from me into its hollow.

The womb is a semipermeable membrane, and an echo,
a voice that hears what it calls.

You made me while I made you; nothing is owed. I came
to the canyon rim and saw

how best to carry you: I let the stone go.

Watershed

Train out of Altoona

You are taking the train. You are taking the train from where you began
and you plan to ride till the end.

In the railroad repair yard, red trolley car barns stenciled with the names
of the old gods, the SAMUEL RAY SHOPS

and the PRR, serried windows chalked white or gapped like bad teeth.
The station was grand before it burned,

its rose window and white limestone salvaged and hauled off at night
to some richer city,

and where you wait now is all prefab walls, one room with one story
set in a tangle of tracks no longer sorted

by trains pulling through. In the yard, locomotives rust to rails that go
nowhere, and a candelabra of brick smokestacks

restates the proof of rectangles able to curve into a cylindrical figure
and of the creatures that molted these husks,

but where are they now, and is this all that is left of their history?

~ ~ ~

The whistle blows and the train slips past boarded-up storefronts,
neon signs half-winking on,

the Boyer Candy factory gone dark, the silk mills gone dark; no work,
no workers, no work.

Lakemont Park bounded by chain link, its vast pleasure pool drained
and the lake silting in, its Ferris wheel of bones.

Main Street's crumbling brownstones giving way to peeling-paint
row houses sharing walls and a backyard

piled with oil drums, car parts, and metal bed frames. Where are they,
the people who burned the oil,

drove the cars, made babies in those beds, where are they?

~ ~ ~

Beyond the last house, a low circle of mountains, the world in a blue bowl
you once felt safe in,

cinder swales sloped down from fields frozen in stubble; a thresher's mute
claws, rust-streaked silos

stenciled with hex signs and ads for *Mail Pouch Tobacco* and *Jesus Who Saves*;
Jesus who did not save.

You are on the train from where you began in the years when all ways
led out, and you lean back, soothed

by the hum of time and momentum, but beneath you the cross-ties
have been working loose like teeth

from the moment they first were pinned, and so the engine must slow,
creaking and groaning

and must slow again until you are almost not moving at all, and sometimes
the train stops and then

—you are not imagining this—it begins to move backward.

Election Returns 2016

The way up the mountain was like always:
switchbacks & more switchbacks,
the trail rising through redwoods arced
over a silence rinsed with new rain.
We were in an emerald world
of fern & mist & moss trembled
with tiny glass beads. It was dusk
and late fall. We knew what would happen:
we'd be made to suffer for a few hours
before reaching the summit
then would emerge above the fog.

Yes, there were portents: maple leaves
pasting the trail with bloody handprints,
evergreens brittle & brown,
a few manzanita oddly in bloom.
Lake water like pewter, faint reek of smoke
we hoped came from a controlled burn.
We went on walking the trail
by memory, memory that also held rain
after drought & wild iris massed like stars.

We walked till we came upon what was left
of the deer: a white basket of rib cage
that looked almost human, matted fur,

tags of torn flesh. On the way down,

it would all become clear, but even

then we understood: it was a fresh kill,

and the cougar was close. We looked around

to see who among us was prey

and we understood, then, what would happen.

Sit with Me

Sit again with me by the fire
to debate the placement of commas and italics
and the meanings of words
as if the world were at stake
in this warm, bright room

secured by a heavy door with a good lock
on a street in a block no ICE agent
would dare wield his baton
and that for a moment, what matters is nothing
more than words on this page.

Here in this room, we believe in choosing
the right words, in the right order,
and that it makes a difference
whether *craven* means "crass"
or something more odious

like "openly indifferent to suffering"
—even if both happen to apply,
only one is precisely correct,
and we believe that matters.
After the election, a woman on the bus

cried out while checking her phone.
"Thank God," she said, the bees

are no longer going extinct—they've
been taken off the Endangered List!"
It was not long after that

the EPA was shut down, and the word
criminal amended to mean children
who escape into this country from
earthquakes, machetes, and guns.
So many children crossing those rivers

and last night, workers taken right out
of the kitchen at Cavallo Point, but here
in my neighborhood the magnolias
are unfolding large creamy blooms
with an *abandon* that brings to mind

the words *wanton* and *craven*. Sit with me
again and remind me words matter
as much as the world. Remind me
craven means not *crass*, but *cowardly*,
even if both happen to apply

to our president, and *evil* and *immoral*
are almost always over-the-top
in a poem. Tell me what each term means

and does not mean and what
this particular four-year term means

to the father who worked here for 20 years
and now must leave his family behind,
and tell me how to parse a sentence
that balances weeping with silence,
children with *criminal* and *abandon*,

and president with *craven* and *crass*
and *openly indifferent to suffering,*
immoral, and *evil*—give me
any meaning that makes any sense
and will not allow the reader to choose,
or to turn away.

Little Brown Bat

1.

That you must fall to fly. That you can live two decades or more.
    That you have young like we do, one per year.

That you make a rich milk to feed your pup and to keep it warm,
    fold it between your wings.

That you eat every day half your weight in mosquitoes, found
    by echolocation one winged speck at a time.

That you hibernate in utter torpor, absorbing the fat you've stored,
    a very precise amount.

That you were, on that July night, a shy, soft thing, a vibration
    just brushing my left eyebrow.

That you were once unnumbered as Dante's leaves in the fall.
    That you die from eating the insects

we poison. That you are cut down by wind turbines, the drop
    in air pressure popping you

like kernels of corn. That you swoop and careen arcs traced
    by the streetlights of my childhood summers.

That when my father taught me to swat down a bat with a broom
    —a brown mouse with wings and soft ear tufts—

he cleared his throat and looked away. That you rarely are rabid

        and never drink blood—no, you eat fruit

and, in a day half your weight in mosquitoes—that you grow

        your own and our food, pollinating our orchards.

2.

Magnified, *Geomyces destructans* is branched and fletched

        like a blue snowflake,

and it blooms over your face, body, and wings, etching your flesh

        in terrible symmetry,

and when you most need to be still, it disturbs you, makes you

        move in your sleep, burning the fat

you've stored, a very precise amount that assumes a dormant bat,

        one who does not stir, but you do stir

in your sleep, starve, and fall. Not to fly but to make a thick layer

        on the cave floor, crunched underfoot by cavers

who tell the scientists now beginning to count you, bearing the spores

        on their boots from cave to cave.

3.

That you starve in your sleep in such numbers you tuft a carpet of plush,
        then bones, that in trying to save you

we only spread the disease. That it takes twelve months to gestate
        and wean one pup. That in a single cave and year

your number fell from a quarter million to thirty-five bats—make that
        thirty-four, less tonight's shy, soft vibration

near my left eyebrow, swatted by reflex, that sank like a small, tangled kite
        into the toilet behind me.

That, when afraid, we revert to lessons taught in our childhood;
        we shrink from the least vibration of our air,

we plug our ears and close our eyes against any flailing; we look away
        from what we've been taught we can't bear,

we avert our gaze, and when we can, we flush it away.

Blame

the olive tree that dropped its great gout
of dark fruit onto asphalt, for the swerve
and spinout etched in fresh virgin press;
blame the natural law that made helpless
bodies attract and collide then come to rest
in the acacia-treed canyon. The driver sat
behind the wheel, side not pierced—not yet.
Yes he was drunk, but only with joy
for the lovely lithe boy now fused with the car,
shrink-wrapped in leather and steel
and veiled by the webbed windshield; the boy
who sang backup gospel like a bruised angel
and was the hope of his whole Bronx block.
Blame the last bright note that opened his throat
and sank into pollen and dust.

Vehicular

You were sure it was only a deer, dead
the second we hit it, so we didn't stop
but pressed on for Orlando

and never spoke of it again, not once
in forty years. It was near dawn
on the Georgia Interstate, you driving

all night in sheeting sleet and rain.
There was a blow, or not, then he was down
—splayed, long-limbed, and already past—

it happened so fast I thought I'd dreamt
the pale vertical slice of his face
between ice-clabbered wipers, the shudder

under the tires, first front, then back.
But I was wrong. The dreaming came later.

Iconostasis

on the YouTube video examination of the body of Hamza Ali Al-Khateeb,
13, tortured and killed by the Syrian government

For the plastic parted and peeled back to reveal him,
a panel woven in linen.

For his hands, a hummingbird's thrum and blur.
For his arm lifted up

by the latex-gloved hand, water poured past all thirst.
For the gloved hand,

the pale, powdery fingers of a terrible angel. For each
thumbprint bruise,

the petal of a dark rose. For his voice calling his mother,
the single note of a thrush.

For where they burned him, a choir of stars tangling
a high, unresolved chord.

For his round child's face, the low sough of an oboe.
For his eyes, a palm

to stroke them closed. A close-up to anoint orbital bone,
brow, mouth, and chin;

Vaseline on the lens; a finger in ash to write his name.

Guernica

Do you still look and see that it is good?
You spoke, then saw what you'd wrought.
We are the monster in the mirror, God,

your world made of words. *Let there be* untied
sky, earth and sea, and night from light,
and you looked and saw it was good.

With spit and a fistful of dust, you made
the first man. Then to make Eve, took him apart.
You made everything, even the mirror, God,

and it's all carnage. A cell cleaves to breed.
Before one war ends, the next one will start,
then the next—still looking? Still good?—

and the eyes that weep for spilled blood
are set in a head that plots the next slaughter.
A monster. Picasso's vexed mirror. O God,

how will you judge the quick and the dead
when the dead include this child for a martyr?
Can you really still look and say it is good?
The monster *and* the mirror—it's all you, God.

The Bugler Responds to Mary

after *Annunciation*, by Upper Rhenish Master,
also Congressman Todd Akin's public remarks about "legitimate rape"

What will He do, slut, if you refuse? He will silence your voice,
break your reed, have you stripped

and flayed. Make you my mute, my spit rag, my instrument case,
merely a vessel to swell, split, and spill fruit.

Without God, what water, what soil, what salt, what sun?
I, mouthpiece, claim absolution

and absolute reign under his reign. Have you seen how a trumpet
is made? Silver stamped thin,

rolled and bent, crimped like a thread. God does that with breath,
and absent his breath all song is scattered,

broken like chaff across his long staff. We all live at his sufferance,
and you, you are the pear-shaped note

he allows me to choose—or not—to blow. If it is really rape,
then you will not ripen. If you refuse,

I could teach you the blat-blat interval between bravado and fear,
but it's moot, my dear girl, already done—

He spoke, and I blared into your ear—a son.

Blackout

When the lights went out, a soft silence settled
over everything like fine, heavy ash.
We stopped talking, newly aware of the candles
lit on the table, the edge of everything
blurred in a way that felt beautiful.
We turned off our phones to conserve the charge
—that was before the towers went down—
and then we looked up from them
into each other's faces. We had not looked before,
not that night. The candlelight
cast different shadows, sculpting ridges and planes
we had not known were there.
Small sounds became acute: a plinking faucet
somewhere, crickets, calls of owls.
We lowered our voices, exposed in darkness
in a way we were never exposed
in the light. Is it wishful thinking to remember
we were kinder with one another then?
There was fear, yes, elemental fear, mineral fear
of the dark and the fire raging 30 miles
to the north. There was fear of showing our fear,
and of showing a certain lack of gratitude
that things were not yet quite dire.
There was the car's gas tank on empty

and the go-bag not yet packed,

the single corridor out already unspooling

a bright red mylar ribbon of traffic

through the dark hills, and above them,

the stars we'd forgotten, usually masked

by the streetlights but tonight bright,

cold, unperturbed, still there

throwing fire at our eyes from light years away.

How funny, to measure distance with time.

Or maybe, not funny at all: it takes five minutes

to make the freeway in no traffic, an hour

or more during rush hour to quit the county,

the precise distance between life and death

or was for the cars caught in the hell

called Paradise, sparks arcing like sequins

across windshields, steering wheels too hot

to touch, flames walling both sides.

Some people died in their cars, or running

from them, or in their beds or barns

where they'd gone to let out the horses.

Moments before, maybe

sitting at a table like this in the new dark,

looking around at each other in wonder,

seeing something new, and listening, really listening.

Watershed

If the egret and heron are woodblock prints,
these wildly outsized birds are whole canvases
palette-knifed in titanium, a descended
cumulus. They flock the sandbar and float,
a yellow bill folded along each curving neck.

A beak tips to swallow, and a star un-pleats
cinnabar against azure sky. I walk close, but
the birds take no notice. We come,
we shrink the marshland, we save the marshland,
we continue to poison the marshland.

Have you seen the columns at Sagrada Família?
Porphyry, granite, basalt. Our redwoods were cut
a century ago. But so long as what's overlooked
can breed life in a puddle, it seems, the birds will come,
and I am for the moment deaf bliss to the voice inside,

novice in a convent of silence belled by the calls
of many birds. Consecrated, seeing such a fortune
of great white pelican as I did not imagine existed;
here, along a frontage road wedged between
the Royal Coach Car Wash and the Town Center Mall.

I Learn to Field Strip an M-16

Driving through the Poconos in late fall;
flash storm with actual thunder and lightning
not seen since I fled west 40 years ago,
my cheap rental a thin beer can hydroplaning
past scarlets and golds against a rinsed sky.
Bite in the air, dark edge on the sun
then down, down into the gray, fraying holler
past rusted train tracks and Confederate flags
and *Jesus Saves* signs chalked on old barns
to visit the sister who soon will have forgotten
my name. Her husband, a Vietnam War vet
whose M-16 hangs above the mantle
is a good man who will stand by her.

I did not bring up his email the week before
explaining how tree huggers are to blame
for our terrible wildfires, but instead,
remembering some war documentary,
asked about the machine guns that jammed.
Firing residue, he said, some tiny rod
the government had neglected to send,
or send on time, or to the right place.
*When a gun got slugged, the fix was chuck it
into a rice paddy*, and, taking his own gun

down from the wall, *I'll tell you what, this*
is what stood between me and death.

When he showed me how to field-strip the M-16,
the first thing he did was yank a lever back
and eject what looked like a live round
onto the sofa. I'd never touched a gun before
though I'd seen many, in glass safes next to the bed,
in racks on cars, on straps over shoulders,
or held like a child by men sitting around the table
after dinner, men who sometimes also held
a sleeping child.

At first, I wouldn't touch it but only watched,
keeping myself pure and above it all
like when my dad, in the last year
of his truly deplorable illness—the lung disease
that killed my and most of my friends' parents—
visited my law firm on the 33rd floor.
After he left, everyone joked they could see him
a mile down Market Street on account of his blazer:
an eye-shattering rust-and-green-neon plaid.

We stayed awhile, floating above the world
in that steel-and-glass box with its deep carpets

and dark exotic wood walls. It was his best jacket,

purchased at great expense to him, and he wore it

to look good so he would not embarrass me.

The joking was gentle but still stemmed from contempt

and the self I most despise is the one

who thinks she's above it all—more pure, or better,

or smarter than everyone and everywhere she came from

—who, when those lawyers laughed, laughed too.

Epitaph after Vallejo

Late afternoon is the time I would choose:
shadows steeped deep and purple, the lake
mauve—the very air mauve—a shade of ache
like the sky blooming its own demise.
When I die, let it be late July, humid blur
of leaves starry with pollen, no wind
to stir the origami of green, the blind
folds listless in the light's last fat golden pour.

Rebecca Foust has died. In and out of her time,
she longed to arc meteor, loom large with myth
—and fell short. Only One-Great-Book shy
of epic she entered the dirt, her last, best rhyme
made flesh in her own issue; a skeptic
of the language of living, and its aftermath.

Dream of the Rood, Reprise

On me are the wounds seen
"THE DREAM OF THE ROOD"

You should follow your dream, whispered the rude

young yoga instructor, earnest, and bent

on proving that pain could, at its heart, be good,

and that I ached from more than this hardwood

floor against my spine's misalignment. I'd signed

up to follow it—my dream—but now I rued

the day I'd moved to this crazy state, loaded

with cord-stack: the family tree felled

by blood, smoke, and gin. My parents died

years before they each died. Light was divided

from light in every small pane, so I went

west. Burnt was the dream-shape of home, root

shaft, and crossbeam. In my first year of dead

and no weather, I wanted winter; I pined

for trees with no leaves and for any word

spoken in tongues. *Stand,* she said, *on your head,*

and it began to rain. Outside, upside down,

a tree bled. I dreamt blurred redbud, the rood,

pane-pierced light, a dead tree in luminous bloom.

The Fox

Maybe if we hadn't interlocked our gene sets
like so many Legos, my children would have suffered
less, or maybe I'd have no children at all

and wouldn't have stopped leaving home at dawn
to catch the ferry to the city to defend pop stars
and Armani suits with big ideas about finance.

No, I'd have traveled the world, tried that Japanese dish
that either kills you or gives you an orgasm, gone
bungee-jumping in Australia, river rafting in Brazil,

maybe married a musician or artist instead of a man
who scans sports stats the way poets scan lines,
or not married at all, with many lovers instead,

or maybe switched jobs, working against Apartheid,
fracking, genital mutilation, or war. Maybe saved
a rainforest, or one narrow strip of wetland next to a mall.

But then I'd have missed the years of waking to your eyes,
blue and always already open. And summers at the Cape,
our son's all-night vigil for the cabbage moths

hatched by bad luck or bad genes, or maybe just hatched
as they were meant to there inside the porch lantern,
so they could be rescued one winged speck at a time,

me beside him on the old camp blanket, fighting sleep
to count the Perseids wheeling overhead, one for every
whispered one-one-thousand, two-one-thousand

then waking at dead low tide to world-withdrawn silence
damp with salt and new earth, and hearing again
what woke me—the fox sobbing somewhere in the marsh—
and she sounded glad.

NOTES

"Only" owes a debt to Stanley Kunitz.

"the unexploded ordnance bin": The Liberty Ship S.S. James Longstreet anchored off Wellfleet, Massachusetts was used for target practice until about 1970, and beachcombers still find live ordnance often enough that the local police, for a number of years, maintained a bin for its disposal and controlled detonation.

"Everything Golden Is Spilled" is for friend, poet, and mother-in-arms Connie Post.

"Like Birders": As neurodivergence becomes less pathologized, people are beginning to understand that many so-called "disabilities"—things like hyper-focus and extreme detail-orientation are, or can be, strengths.

The epigraph in "Prompt" is a paraphrase of a remark made by Stephen Dunn at a reading at Francesca Bell's house in northern California about a decade ago.

"Lines": "Redline" was the last name of my mother and grandmother and is not meant here to refer to the discriminatory racist practice of withholding home-loan funds or insurance from neighborhoods considered poor economic risks.

"Blame": I was on the defense team in People v. Vandross, the vehicular manslaughter case that inspired this poem. Luthor Vandross was accused—unjustly and for political reasons—of vehicular manslaughter for the death of a passenger riding in his car during an accident; the charges were eventually dismissed.

"Iconostasis": An iconostasis is an altar screen meant to shield congregants from direct vision of God. The idea is that we are able to see the divine more clearly when our vision is obscured; a direct view is more than human seeing can handle and also is disrespectful. There are at least three such screens in the poem. First is the computer screen, which allows viewers to view horrors at a remove. Second is the consciously-adorned poetic language, which operates like the "Vaseline on the lens" of a camera. The third is the actual video camera itself, which adds another layer of screening that would not be present if the viewer were actually in the room watching the examination.

ACKNOWLEDGMENTS

Thank you to the following journals and anthologies who have previously published some of these poems:

Academy of American Poets, *Poem-a-Day*; *Alaska Quarterly Review*; *American Literary Review*; *Arts & Letters*; *Birmingham Poetry Review*; *Concho River Review*; *Cortland Review*; *Hudson Review*; *Massachusetts Review*; *Mid-American Review*; *Mom Egg Review*; *Narrative Magazine*; *Nimrod*; *North American Review*; *Poet Lore*; *Poetry East*, *Poetry International*; *Prairie Schooner*; *Salamander*; *Seattle Review*; *Sewanee Review*; *Southern Indiana Review*; *Southwest Review*; *Thirty-Two Poems*; and *Zyzzyva*.

"Abeyance" appeared in *How Lovely the Ruins* (Spiegel & Grau 2017), *Healing the Divide: Poems of Kinship and Connection* (Green Writers Press 2019), James Crews, ed., *Zoom In: Individual and Society* (Schöningh Verlag 2017), the *Huffington Post* 11/19/16, "18 Compassionate Poems to Help You Weather Uncertain Times," and was featured on *The Slowdown* on 2/5/20.

"reflection" appears in the anthology *Alongside We Travel: Contemporary Poets on Autism* (NYQ Books 2018), Sean Thomas Dougherty, ed.

"Night Skating" was reprinted in *Nostos*, Vol. 2 No. 2 (2018).

"Dream of the Rood, Reprise," "exsultate jubilate," and "Paean" were reprinted in *Poetry Daily* on 10/2/14, 8/15/16, and 12/1/15

"the unexploded ordnance bin" was reprinted in *Verse Daily* on 9/25/19.

The following poems appear in *The Unexploded Ordnance Bin*, winner of the 2018 Swan Scythe Press Chapbook Contest: "the unexploded ordnance

bin," "reflection," "Perseids, "Everything Golden Is Spilled," "Echo," "Little
   Brown Bat," "Blame," "Iconostasis," and "Abeyance."
"Blackout" and "Sit with Me" won the 2020 Pablo Neruda Prize judged by
   Kaveh Akbar. "Lines" won 2018 Poetry International's CP Cavafy Prize.
   "Iconostasis" won the 2015 James Hearst Prize judged by Jane Hirshfield.
Thanks to the editors of the following reviews for nominating these poems
   for the Pushcart Prize: *Arts & Letters* ("Collaborator"), *Poet Lore*
   ("Dream of the Rood"), *The Hudson Review* ("Like Birders").
Thank you to my family and friends, without whose support I could
   not have written these poems, especially the writer with me from the
   beginning, Jasmin Darznik. Thanks to fellow pod members Buffie
   Ballard, Toni Piccinini, and Brad O'Connell for getting me through
   COVID-19 quarantine and for always having my back. I am grateful
   to the many readers of this manuscript, including Peter Campion,
   Tom Centolella, Susan Griffin, Bill Harvey, Annie Kim, Julia Levine,
   Carolyn Miller, Albert Flynn de Silva, Susan Terris, and Javier Zamora.
   I also appreciate the many first readers of these poems, including Susan
   Browne, Susan Cohen, Julia Levine, and Jeanne Wagner, and a much
   longer list in Tom Centolella's monthly poetry workshop. Thanks to
   my teachers, especially Ruth Beck and Linda Watanabe McFerrin, and
   to Warren Wilson for the excellence and rigor of its MFA program.
   Gratitude, always, to Smith College for giving this scholarship student
   the chance that changed my life. I'm also grateful to the residencies and
   conferences whose grants supported the writing of these poems: The
   Frost Place, Hedgebrook, MacDowell, Sewanee, and West Chester.
   Finally, huge thanks to Martha Rhodes and the crew at Four Way
   Books for believing in my book and for edits that were crucial as well as
   inspiring and supportive.

ABOUT THE AUTHOR

Rebecca Foust is the author of *Paradise Drive* (Press 53, 2015), winner of the Press 53 Award for Poetry and the Poetry Society of Virginia Book Award; *All That Gorgeous Pitiless Song* (Many Mountains Moving, 2010), winner of the Many Mountains Moving Book Prize; and *God, Seed: Poetry & Art about the Natural World* (Tebot Bach, 2010), a collaboration with artist Lorna Stevens that won the Foreword Book of the Year Award for Poetry. Her chapbooks are *The Unexploded Ordnance Bin* (Swan Scythe Press, 2020) winner of the Swan Scythe Chapbook Award, and *Mom's Canoe* (Texas Review Press 2009) and *Dark Card* (Texas Review Press 2008), winners of the Robert Phillips Poetry Prize in consecutive years. Foust's poems appear widely, in *The Hudson Review, Narrative, Ploughshares, POETRY, The Southern Review,* and elsewhere. Recognitions include the 2020 Pablo Neruda Prize for Poetry judged by Kaveh Akbar, the C.P. Cavafy and James Hearst Poetry Prizes, a 2017-19 Marin County Poet Laureateship, and fellowships from The Frost Place, Hedgebrook, MacDowell, and Sewanee Writers' Conference.

PUBLICATION OF THIS BOOK WAS MADE POSSIBLE BY GRANTS AND DONATIONS. WE ARE ALSO GRATEFUL TO THOSE INDIVIDUALS WHO PARTICIPATED IN OUR 2021 BUILD A BOOK PROGRAM. THEY ARE:

Anonymous (16), Maggie Anderson, Susan Kay Anderson, Kristina Andersson, Kate Angus, Kathy Aponick, Sarah Audsley, Jean Ball, Sally Ball, Clayre Benzadón, Greg Blaine, Laurel Blossom, adam bohannon, Betsy Bonner, Lee Briccetti, Joan Bright, Jane Martha Brox, Susan Buttenwieser, Anthony Cappo, Carla and Steven Carlson, Paul and Brandy Carlson, Renee Carlson, Alice Christian, Karen Rhodes Clarke, Mari Coates, Jane Cooper, Ellen Cosgrove, Peter Coyote, Robin Davidson, Kwame Dawes, Michael Anna de Armas, Brian Komei Dempster, Renko and Stuart Dempster, Matthew DeNichilo, Rosalynde Vas Dias, Kent Dixon, Patrick Donnelly, Lynn Emanuel, Blas Falconer, Elliot Figman, Jennifer Franklin, Helen Fremont and Donna Thagard, Gabriel Fried, John Gallaher, Reginald Gibbons, Jason Gifford, Jean and Jay Glassman, Dorothy Tapper Goldman, Sarah Gorham and Jeffrey Skinner, Lauri Grossman, Julia Guez, Sarah Gund, Naomi Guttman and Jonathan Mead, Kimiko Hahn, Mary Stewart Hammond, Beth Harrison, Jeffrey Harrison, Melanie S. Hatter, Tom Healy and Fred Hochberg, K.T. Herr, Karen Hildebrand, Joel Hinman, Deming Holleran, Lillian Howan, Thomas and Autumn Howard, Catherine Hoyser, Elizabeth Jackson, Jessica Jacobs and Nickole Brown, Christopher Johanson, Jen Just, Maeve Kinkead, Alexandra Knox, Lindsay and John Landes, Suzanne Langlois, Laura Lauth, Sydney Lea, David Lee and Jamila Trindle, Rodney Terich Leonard, Jen Levitt, Howard Levy, Owen Lewis, Matthew Lippman, Jennifer Litt, Karen Llagas, Sara London and Dean Albarelli, Clarissa Long, James

Longenbach, Cynthia Lowen, Ralph and Mary Ann Lowen, Ricardo Maldonado, Myra Malkin, Jacquelyn Malone, Carrie Mar, Kathleen McCoy, Ellen McCulloch-Lovell, Lupe Mendez, David Miller, Josephine Miller, Nicki Moore, Guna Mundheim, Matthew Murphy and Maura Rockcastle, Michael and Nancy Murphy, Myra Natter, Jay Baron Nicorvo, Ashley Nissler, Kimberly Nunes, Rebecca and Daniel Okrent, Robert Oldshue and Nina Calabresi, Kathleen Ossip, Judith Pacht, Cathy McArthur Palermo, Marcia and Chris Pelletiere, Sam Perkins, Susan Peters and Morgan Driscoll, Patrick Phillips, Robert Pinsky, Megan Pinto, Connie Post, Kyle Potvin, Grace Prasad, Kevin Prufer, Alicia Jo Rabins, Anna Duke Reach, Victoria Redel, Martha Rhodes, Paula Rhodes, Louise Riemer, Sarah Santner, Amy Schiffman, Peter and Jill Schireson, Roni and Richard Schotter, James and Nancy Shalek, Soraya Shalforoosh, Peggy Shinner, Anita Soos, Donna Spruijt-Metz, Ann F. Stanford, Arlene Stang, Page Hill Starzinger, Marina Stuart, Yerra Sugarman, Marjorie and Lew Tesser, Eleanor Thomas, Tom Thompson and Miranda Field, James Tjoa, Ellen Bryant Voigt, Connie Voisine, Moira Walsh, Ellen Dore Watson, Calvin Wei, John Wender, Eleanor Wilner, Mary Wolf, and Pamela and Kelly Yenser.